bryc

BLAZERS

Wild Outdoors

Fly Fishing

by Cindy Jenson-Elliott

Reading Consultant: Barbara J. Fox
Reading Specialist
North Carolina State University

Content Consultant:
Matt Wilhelm
Yellowstone Fly Fishing School
Livingston, Montana

CAPSTONE PRESS
a capstone imprint

Blazers is published by Capstone Press,
151 Good Counsel Drive, P.O. Box 669, Mankato, Minnesota 56002.
www.capstonepub.com

 Books published by Capstone Press are manufactured with paper
containing at least 10 percent post-consumer waste.

Library of Congress Cataloging-in-Publication Data
Jenson-Elliott, Cynthia L.
  Fly fishing / by Cindy Jenson-Elliott.
    p. cm. — (Blazers. wild outdoors)
  Includes bibliographical references and index.
  Summary: "Describes the equipment, skills, and techniques needed for fly fishing"—Provided by
publisher.
  ISBN 978-1-4296-4811-0 (library binding)
  1. Fly fishing—Juvenile literature. I. Title.
  SH456.J464 2012
  799.1'1—dc22   2011003781

Editorial Credits

Angie Kaelberer, editor; Bobbie Nuytten, designer; Sarah Schuette, photo stylist;
    Marcy Morin, scheduler; Eric Manske, production specialist

Photo Credits

Capstone Studio: Karon Dubke, 14–15; Getty Images: Image Studios, 12–13; iStockphoto:
Douglas Allen, 18–19, Joe Michl, 16–17, 26–27, Julie Kendall, 18 (front), Sean Boggs, 4–5, 6–7;
Newscom: Design Pics/Corey Hochachka, 24–25, 29, Ingram Publishing, 16 (front), Zuma Press/
s70, 8–9; Shutterstock: BW Folsom, 10 (left), Dan Bannister, 10–11, James Coleman, 20–21,
Pavol Kmeto, 12 (left), 22–23, Timurpix, cover

Artistic Effects

Capstone Studio: Karon Dubke (woods); Shutterstock: rvika (wood), rvrspb (fence),
VikaSuh (sign)

Printed in the United States of America in Stevens Point, Wisconsin.
032011   006111WZF11

Table of Contents

Chapter 1

Fooling a Trout

You are fly fishing in a clear, fast-moving stream. You **cast** your fishing line into the water. A hungry trout is swimming nearby.

cast—to throw a fishing line and hook out into the water

Wild Fact:

Fly fishers catch trout and bass in freshwater, and tuna and snapper in saltwater.

5

Wild Fact:

When a fish bites, fishers set the hook in the fish's mouth by lifting the rod and pulling in the line.

6

Your **fly** skims the water. The trout thinks it is a real insect. Snap! He bites. Pop! You set the hook. You got him!

fly—a fishing lure made to look like an insect or other fish food

Chapter 2

Rods, Flies, and Line

Fly fishing rods are long, strong, and flexible. Most rods are made of **graphite** or **fiberglass**. Reels attached to the rods hold the fishing line.

graphite—a strong, lightweight material made from a gray or black mineral

fiberglass—a strong, lightweight material made from thin threads of glass

Wild Fact:

Fly fishing rods can be 15 feet (4.6 meters) long or longer.

Fly fishers use different flies to catch different fish. A hook is hidden in each fly.

fly

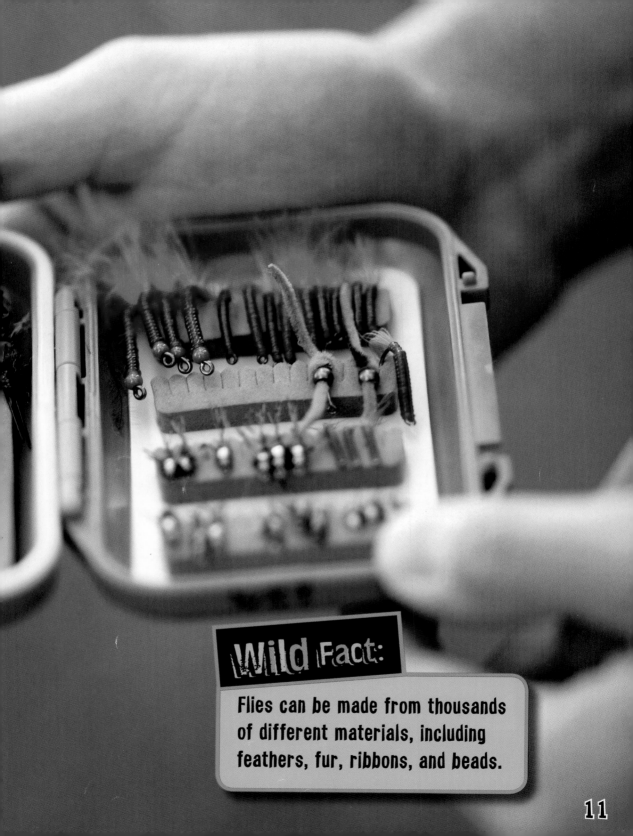

Fly fishing line comes in different weights. Heavy line sinks to carry flies below the surface of the water. Lightweight line allows flies to float on top of the water. A clear **leader** connects the line to the fly.

leader—a length of thin line that fly fishers tie to their flies

Leader

Wild Fact:

Fishers often use an improved clinch knot to fasten the leader to the fly.

wading staff

fishing hat

fly fishing rod

flies

leader

hooks

tying glue

fly box

needle nose pliers

clippers

vest

fly fishing line

fly fishing reel

14

Fly Fishing Equipment

fishing rod case

waders

net

sunglasses

fishing license

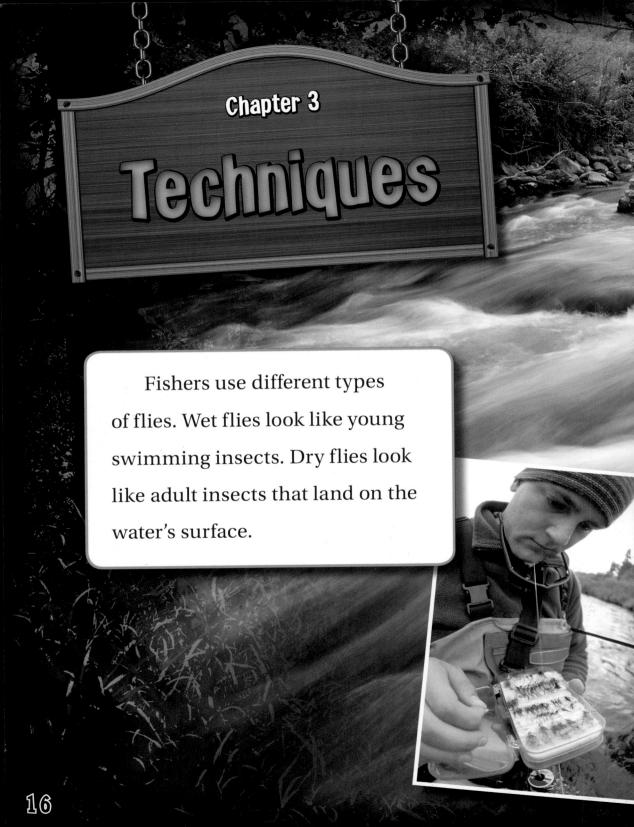

Chapter 3

Techniques

Fishers use different types of flies. Wet flies look like young swimming insects. Dry flies look like adult insects that land on the water's surface.

Wild Fact:

Many fly fishers spend the winter making new flies to use in the spring and summer.

Casting a fly line takes practice. Fly fishers use both hands to fish. One hand holds the rod. The other hand controls the line.

Wild Fact:

Fishers often wade into the water to cast. Waders help keep them dry.

waders—tall waterproof boots or a chest-high, waterproof garment with attached boots

19

Fishers want to sneak up on f
Fishers often wear colors that ble
with their surroundings.

Wild Fact:

Fish can feel the vibrations
of people walking at the
edge of a riverbank.

Fly fishers watch how real fish prey moves. They try to make the flies look alive. Fishers **dap** and **skate** the flies across the water's surface.

dap—to let the fly bounce on the water from a short line

skate—to cast the fly across the top of the water

Chapter 4

Safety

Wading alone or in strong **currents** is dangerous. Fishers keep their balance by taking small, slow steps into the water.

current—the movement of water in a river, stream, or ocean

Wild Fact:

Wading staffs help fishers judge water depth and current speed.

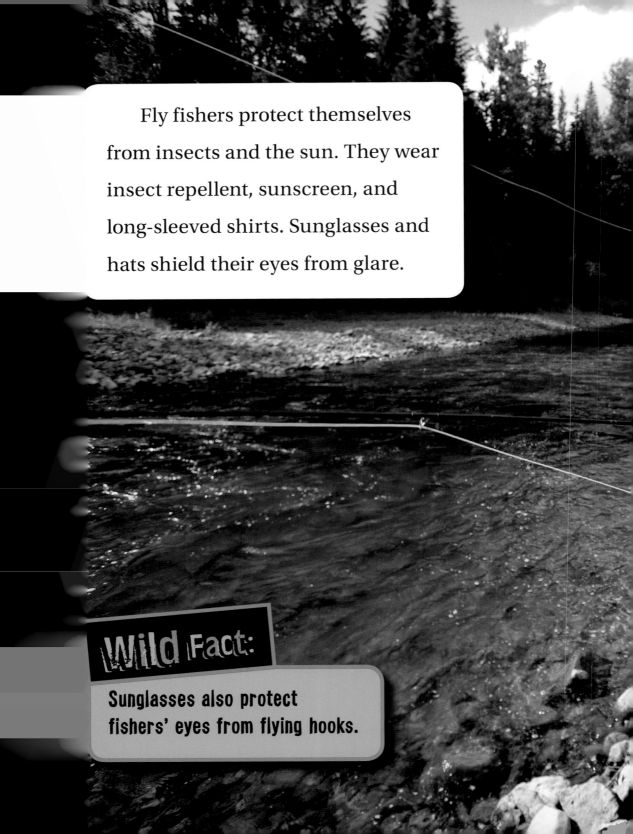

Fly fishers protect themselves from insects and the sun. They wear insect repellent, sunscreen, and long-sleeved shirts. Sunglasses and hats shield their eyes from glare.

Wild Fact:

Sunglasses also protect fishers' eyes from flying hooks.

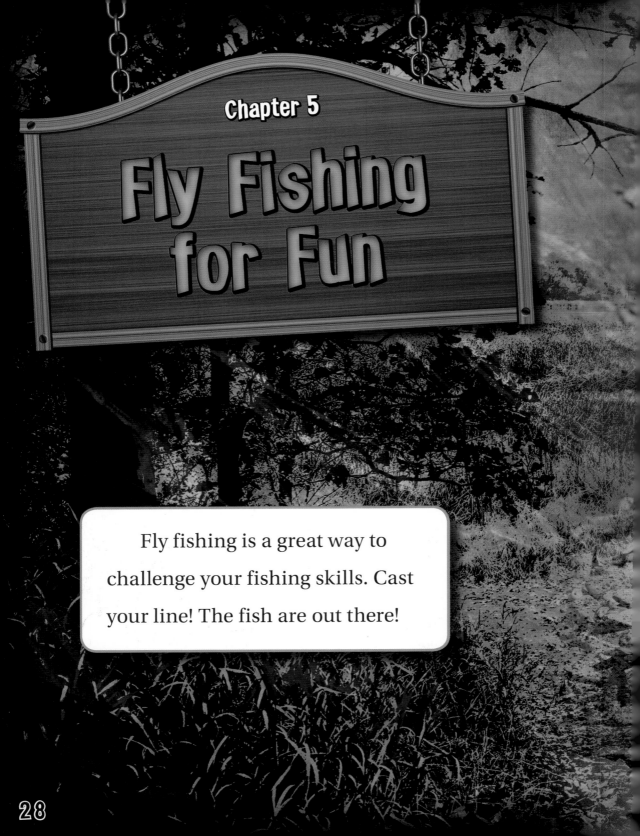

Chapter 5

Fly Fishing for Fun

Fly fishing is a great way to challenge your fishing skills. Cast your line! The fish are out there!

Glossary

cast (KAST)—to throw a fishing line and hook out into the water

current (KUHR-uhnt)—the movement of water in a river, ocean, or stream

dap (DAP)—to let the fly bounce on the water from a short line

fiberglass (FYE-buhr-glas)— a strong, lightweight material made from thin threads of glass

fly (FLY)—a fishing lure made to look like an insect or other fish food

graphite (GRAF-ite)—a strong, lightweight material made from a gray or black mineral

leader (LEE-duhr)—a length of thin line that fly fishers tie to their flies

skate (SKAYT)—to cast the fly across the top of the water

waders (WAY-durz)—tall waterproof boots or a chest-high, waterproof garment with attached boots

Read More

Ford, Martin. *Fishing.* Master This! New York: PowerKids Press, 2010.

Hopkins, Ellen. *Fly Fishing.* The Great Outdoors. Mankato, Minn.: Capstone Press, 2008.

Lindeen, Carol K. *Freshwater Fishing.* Wild Outdoors. Mankato, Minn.: Capstone Press, 2011.

Newman, Gary. *Fishing.* Crabtree Contact. New York: Crabtree Publishing, 2009.

Internet Sites

FactHound offers a safe, fun way to find Internet sites related to this book. All of the sites on FactHound have been researched by our staff.

Here's all you do:

Visit *www.facthound.com*

Type in this code: 9781429648110

Index